Música Latina para dos 1

6 Late Elementary Piano Duets That Celebrate Latin American Styles

Wynn-Anne Rossi

Latin America, including Central and South America, has produced some of the most captivating music in history! Perhaps it is because this music is a product of many cultures. Africans, Europeans, and indigenous people have come together to create unique musical styles that use rhythmic syncopations, colorful harmonies, and mesmerizing melodies.

In the *Música Latina* series, students experience the rhythms, styles, and musical characteristics of Latin American music while exploring the history and culture of this part of the world. Each duet begins with short rhythm exercises in the *primo* and *secondo* that prepare students for the rhythm patterns featured in the piece. A brief description of each title helps spark the performers' imaginations. Through the music in Book 1, late elementary students will celebrate the sounds of Latin music—*Música Latina*.

Wynn-Anne Rossi

Contents

Alfred Music
P.O. Box 10003
Van Nuys, CA 91410-0003
alfred.com

D1366952

ISBN-10: 1-4706-2303-X
ISBN-13: 978-1-4706-2303-6
Cover Illustration:
Mexican-themed pattern: © Shutterstock.com / mattasbestos

¡Saludos!

"Greetings!"

Homes in Paraguay have no door-bells. Visitors announce their arrival by clapping their hands. With hot weather and open windows, the claps are easy to hear!

Rhythm Workshop

Tap rhythm 3x daily.

mm. 1–5

Secondo

Wynn-Anne Rossi

¡Saludos!

"Greetings!"

Homes in Paraguay have no door-bells. Visitors announce their arrival by clapping their hands. With hot weather and open windows, the claps are easy to hear!

Rhythm Workshop

Tap rhythm 3x daily.

mm. 6–10

Primo

Wynn-Anne Rossi

Spirited (♩ = 208)

Both hands one octave higher than written throughout

La Selva de Iwokrama

"Iwokrama Rain Forest"

One amazing highlight of the mysterious Iwokrama Rain Forest in Guyana is the "Canopy Walkway." The area is filled with chirps from the birdlife, and jaguars can often be spotted with the help of a trained specialist.

Rhythm Workshop

Tap rhythm 3x daily.

mm. 20–23

Secondo

Mysteriously (♩ = 92)

Wynn-Anne Rossi

Both hands one octave lower than written throughout

Rhythm Workshop

Tap rhythm 3x daily.

mm. 24–27

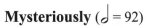

La Selva de Iwokrama

"Iwokrama Rain Forest"

One amazing highlight of the mysterious Iwokrama Rain Forest in Guyana is the "Canopy Walkway." The area is filled with chirps from the birdlife, and jaguars can often be spotted with the help of a trained specialist.

Primo

Mysteriously (♩ = 92)

Both hands one octave higher than written throughout

Wynn-Anne Rossi

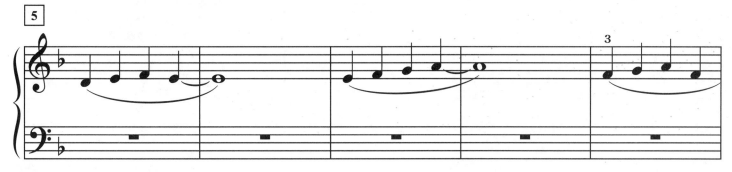

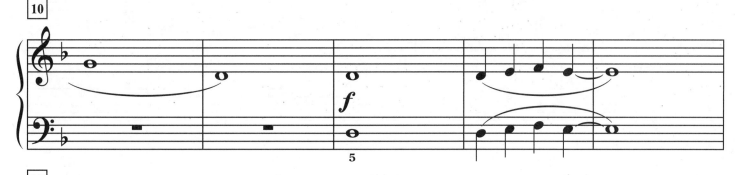

Rumba en la Habana

"Rumba in Havana"

Rumba is a family of rhythms linked to both music and dance that originated in Cuba. The name comes from the Spanish word "rumbo," which means party. Havana is the capital city of Cuba.

Rhythm Workshop

Tap rhythm 3x daily.

mm. 23–26

Secondo

Playfully (♩ = 112)

Both hands one octave lower than written throughout

Wynn-Anne Rossi

Rumba en la Habana

"Rumba in Havana"

Rumba is a family of rhythms linked to both music and dance that originated in Cuba. The name comes from the Spanish word "rumbo," which means party. Havana is the capital city of Cuba.

Rhythm Workshop

Tap rhythm 3x daily.

mm. 7–11

Primo

Wynn-Anne Rossi

Playfully (♩ = 112)

Both hands one octave higher than written throughout

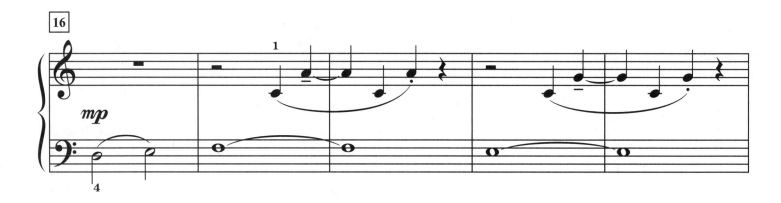

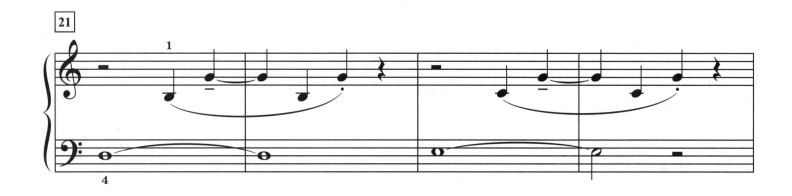

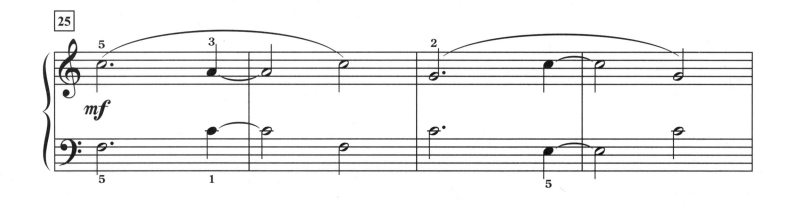

D.C. al Fine

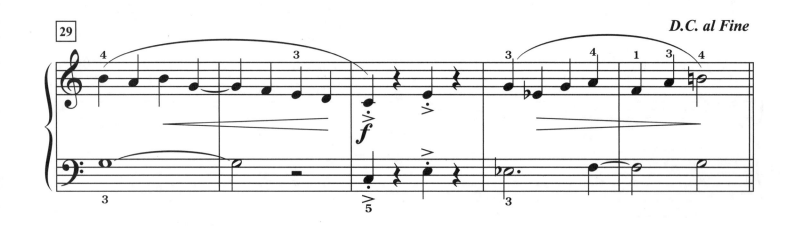

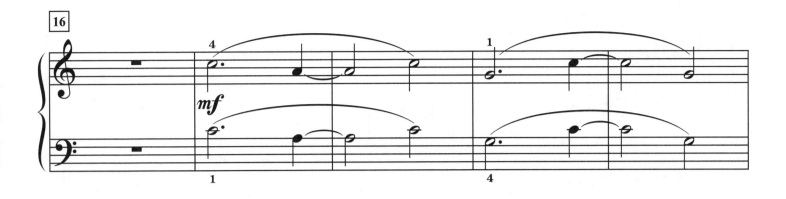

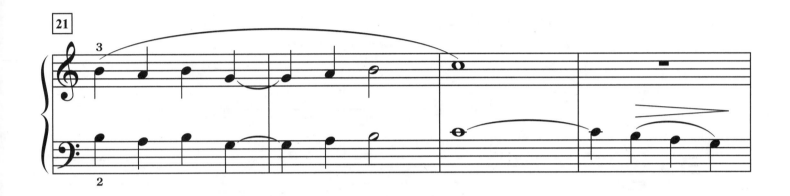

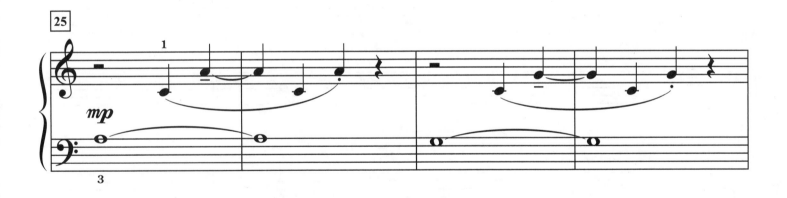

D.C. al Fine

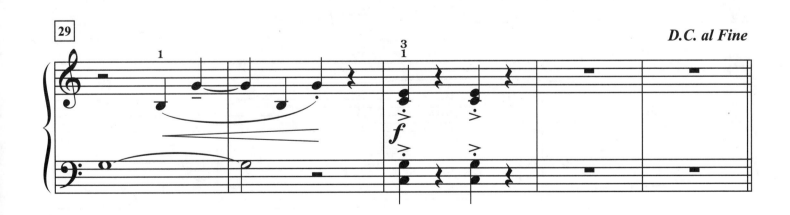

Huayño en las montañas

"Huayño in the Mountains"

Huayño is a genre of popular Peruvian-Andean music and dance that originated in the Andes Mountains of Peru. Certain musical elements have roots that tie back to the former Inca Empire.

Rhythm Workshop

Tap rhythm 3x daily.

mm. 3–6

Secondo

In the spirit of a folk dance ($\downarrow$ = 104)

Both hands one octave lower than written throughout

Wynn-Anne Rossi

Huayño en las montañas

"Huayño in the Mountains"

Huayño is a genre of popular Peruvian-Andean music and dance that originated in the Andes Mountains of Peru. Certain musical elements have roots that tie back to the former Inca Empire.

Wynn-Anne Rossi

Rhythm Workshop

Tap rhythm 3x daily.

mm. 11–14

Primo

In the spirit of a folk dance (♩ = 104)
Both hands one octave higher than written throughout

Secondo

Lago Titicaca

"Lake Titicaca"

The magnificent Lake Titicaca lies in the Andes Mountains on the border of Bolivia and Peru. It is the largest lake in South America and the highest navigated lake in the world. Many cultures consider it sacred.

Rhythm Workshop

Tap rhythm 3x daily.

mm. 17–20

Secondo

Wynn-Anne Rossi

Lago Titicaca

"Lake Titicaca"

The magnificent Lake Titicaca lies in the Andes Mountains on the border of Bolivia and Peru. It is the largest lake in South America and the highest navigated lake in the world. Many cultures consider it sacred.

Rhythm Workshop

Tap rhythm 3x daily.

mm. 17–20

Primo

Wynn-Anne Rossi

Very calm ($\quad$ = 176)

Both hands one octave higher than written throughout

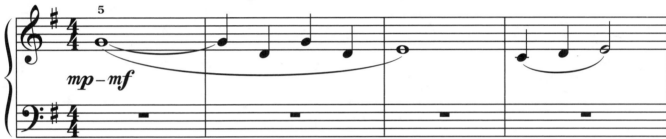

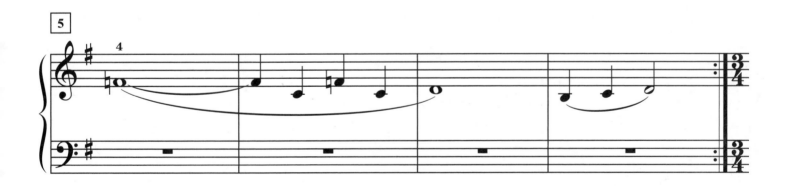

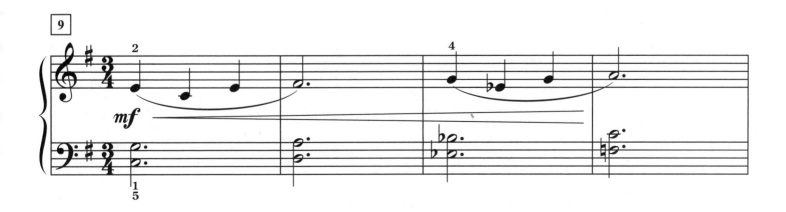

La bomba del Chota

"The Bomba from Chota"

Bomba is an Afro-Ecuadorian dance and music genre that originated in the Chota Valley region of Ecuador. The melodies have prominent Spanish and local influences.

Rhythm Workshop

Tap rhythm 3x daily.

mm. 7–9

Secondo

Energetic! (♩ = 120)

Wynn-Anne Rossi

Both hands one octave lower than written throughout

Rhythm Workshop

Tap rhythm 3x daily.

mm. 1–3

La bomba del Chota

"The Bomba from Chota"

Bomba is an Afro-Ecuadorian dance and music genre that originated in the Chota Valley region of Ecuador. The melodies have prominent Spanish and local influences.

Primo

Energetic! (♩ = 120)

Both hands one octave higher than written throughout

Wynn-Anne Rossi